Praying the Word

From the Book of Philippians

By

L. O. Ovbije

i

ISBN: 978-1-944411-05-3
Copyright © 2020 by Rev. L O. Ovbije

Ovbije World Outreach Ministries, Inc.
P.O. Box 966
Clarkston, GA 30021-0966

Website: owom.org
Email: theword@owom.org

Published by SOIL Foundation, Inc.
P.O. Box 966
Clarkston, GA 30021-0966

All scriptures are from King James Version
(KJV)
Printed in the United States of America.
All rights reserved under International Copyright Law. Contents and/ or cover may not be reproduced in whole or in part in any form, electronic or mechanical, including photocopying, recording, or by any information storage and retrieval system, without the express written consent of the Publisher.

DEDICATION

To God the Father, who love the world he created and sent into the world Jesus Christ his only begotten Son, To Jesus Christ who came into this world in the flesh, died, buried and rose from the dead triumphantly to redeem every human being God created and God made in his own image and likeness, this Jesus Christ of Nazareth has made redemption available for any human being that will trust and believe in him. And to the Holy Spirit, who continueously revealing Jesus Christ to individual and people daily.

I thank God for my dear father who taught me discipline and my precious mother who taught me grace and forgiveness. Both taught me unconditional love. Both love me unconditional.

Pray in the language you speak daily, do not pray to impress people or God. There is no language on earth that is superior to your language. Pray in your own language. Pray in the language you understand, God wants to hear from you now.

I Timothy 3:16

ACKNOWLEDGMENTS

To my wonderful parents, Chief J. E. Ovbije & Mrs. Margaret O.Ovbije, and to my siblings. My father was a man that lived a life that left an excellent and lasting impression on me. My father and mother taught me unconditional love, my mother taught me grace and forgiveness. Our family knew the meaning of a loving, secure and rich home because of my father's presence. I thank God for the private elementary school at Sapele: Children Nursery School, where I attended. It was there that I encounter God for the first time in prayer in a very early age.

To my precious pastor and his lovely wife, both were strong examples of a man and a woman devoted to God. I was fortunate to have pastor & Mrs. Umukoro, both disciples me. I thank them both for their daily early morning prayer life. To the men of God who also impacted my prayer life, W. F. Kumuyi and Benjamin Udi.

Finally to my sweet, precious, wonderful wife Theresa Spearman Ovbije, a woman of God, whom I simply call "sweetie".

CHAPTER ONE

¹ Paul and Timotheus, the servants of Jesus Christ, to all the saints in Christ Jesus which are at Philippi, with the bishops and deacons:

Father in the name of Jesus, I thank you for the body of Christ which is the composition of all believers, Father I thank you that in the body of Christ there is no denomination, there is no ethnicity, there is no male or female, for all believers are one in Christ. Father in the name of Jesus, I bound the spirit of confusion in the body of Christ; I decree unity in the body of Christ, in Jesus name, Amen.

² Grace be unto you, and peace, from God our Father,

and from the Lord Jesus Christ.

Father in the name of Jesus, I thank you for your grace and peace you have given me, I do give your grace and peace that is in me the right of way to dominant me, and by your grace I do give the same grace and peace to others, in Jesus name, Amen.

³ I thank my God upon every remembrance of you,

Father in the name of Jesus, I thank you for who you are, Father I thank you when I think of your goodness in me, Father I thank you for all you did in my life in the past, I thank you for all you are doing in my life in the present, I thank you for all you will be doing in my life in the future, Father I thank you for fellow believers that are living by your word, in Jesus name, Amen.

⁴ Always in every prayer of mine for you all making request with joy,

Father in the name of Jesus, I thank you for the joy of praying for other believers in Christ, I thank you for the grace and joy of interceding for people, in Jesus name, Amen.

⁵ For your fellowship in the gospel from the first day until now;

Father in the name of Jesus, I thank you for the joy of fellowshipping with fellow believers and those that are like precious faith in Christ Jesus, Father I thank you that where two or three are gather together in the name of Jesus, you do faithfully show your present, in Jesus, Amen.

⁶ Being confident of this very thing, that he which hath be-

gun a good work in you will perform it until the day of Jesus Christ:

Father in the name of Jesus, I thank you that I am confident that you that begun a good work in me, will perform it until the day of Jesus Christ, faithful is you that called me, faithful is you that will do it, in Jesus name, Amen.

[7] Even as it is meet for me to think this of you all, because I have you in my heart; inasmuch as both in my bonds, and in the defence and confirmation of the gospel, ye all are partakers of my grace.

Father in the name of Jesus, I thank you for those people who accepted Jesus Christ by the hearing of the gospel of Jesus Christ through me, Father I thank you that you did confirmed the gospel with signs and wonders, Father I pray that they will be establish in you in all things, in Jesus name, Amen.

⁸ For God is my record, how greatly I long after you all in the bowels of Jesus Christ.

Father in the name of Jesus, I pray that those that have accepted Jesus Christ through the ministry you entrusted to me, will grow in grace and faith, Father I pray that they will lead others to Christ, Father I thank you and I rejoice when I think about the ferventness of some of those I led to Christ and those I disciple in the past, Father I am grateful for the working of your Holy Spirit in their lives, in Jesus name, Amen.

⁹ And this I pray, that your love may abound yet more and more in knowledge and in all judgment;

Father in the name of Jesus, I thank you and I pray that the love of those people I have led to Christ may abound more and more in knowledge and in all judgment, Father I pray that the love of all believers in Christ may abound more and more in knowledge and in all judgment, Father I thank you and I pray that my love in Christ will abound more and more in knowledge and in all judgment, I pray that I will walk in wisdom and in discernment, in Jesus name, Amen.

[10] That ye may approve things that are excellent; that ye may be sincere and without offence till the day of Christ.

Father in the name of Jesus, I thank you that your Holy Spirit does abide in me, Father I thank you that your Spirit does lead me to approve things that are excellent, Father I thank you that I am sincere in all things, Father I thank you that I do not hold unto grudges, Father I thank you that I am looking to the soon appearing of your Son Jesus Christ the Great Shepard, and because I do have this hope of Jesus Christ appearance, I do purify myself even as he is pure, in Jesus name, Amen.

11 Being filled with the fruits of righteousness, which are by Jesus Christ, unto the glory and praise of God.

Father in the name of Jesus, I thank you that I am filled with the fruits of righteousness which is by Jesus Christ, I do walk in righteousness, I conduct myself in righteousness, my thoughts are governor by righteousness, in Jesus name, Amen.

12 But I would ye should understand, brethren, that the things which happened unto

me have fallen out rather unto the furtherance of the gospel;

Father in the name of Jesus, I thank you and I know that all things are working together for my good because I love you and because you have called me according to your purpose, in Jesus name, Amen.

13 So that my bonds in Christ are manifest in all the palace, and in all other places;

Father in the name of Jesus, I thank you that my suffering for the sake of Christ is never in vain, Father I thank you that Christ is manifest in my suffering for his name sake, in Jesus name, Amen.

14 And many of the brethren in the Lord, waxing confident by my bonds, are much

more bold to speak the word without fear.

Father in the name of Jesus, I thank you and I pray that whenever I am persecuted for the sake of the gospel, that your grace that is abounding in me will strengthen me, so that I do not draw back but to keep moving forward in you, Father I pray for believers around the world that are suffering persecution that your Holy Spirit will strengthen them with your might, and that they will not draw back but go forward in Christ, in Jesus name, Amen.

[15] Some indeed preach Christ even of envy and strife; and some also of good will:

Father in the name of Jesus, I thank you that some people preach Christ with envy and strife motive, and some preach Christ with good will, Father I pray that I will always preach Christ with your kind of love motive, in Jesus name, Amen.

¹⁶ The one preach Christ of contention, not sincerely, supposing to add affliction to my bonds:

Father in the name of Jesus, I thank you and I pray that your Holy Spirit will convict those who are preaching the gospel with wrong motive, I pray that they will repent of their evil ways, Father I pray you will forgive them and open their eyes to the truth, Father I thank you that it is not your will for any to perish, but that all come to repentance, in Jesus name, Amen.

¹⁷ But the other of love, knowing that I am set for the defence of the gospel.

Father in the name of Jesus, I thank you for those who preach the gospel of Jesus Christ, Father I thank you mostly for the people who preach the gospel of Christ from the motive of love, in Jesus name, Amen.

[18] What then? notwithstanding, every way, whether in pretence, or in truth, Christ is preached; and I therein do rejoice, yea, and will rejoice.

Father in the name Jesus, I thank you for those who preach Christ, Father I thank you for your word said man judge the outward appearance, but you search the heart, Father I thank you that you do know the motive of every human being, Father I thank you that you know the motive of everyone preaching, Father I thank you that you will judge their motives, Father I thank you that the gospel is not bond, in Jesus name, Amen

[19] For I know that this shall turn to my salvation through

your prayer, and the supply of the Spirit of Jesus Christ,

Father in the name of Jesus, I thank you and I pray for those Christians that are suffering for Christ sake and for the gospel of Jesus Christ, that you will strengthen their inner mind with the spirit of might, that they will not be discourage, but stand fast unmovable, always abide in Christ Jesus, in Jesus name, Amen.

[20] According to my earnest expectation and my hope, that in nothing I shall be ashamed, but that with all boldness, as always, so now also Christ shall be magnified in my body, whether it be by life, or by death.

Father in the name of Jesus, I thank you that I am not ashamed of the gospel of Christ, for it is your power unto salvation to everyone who believe, Father I thank you for saving me from this present evil world, in Jesus name, Amen.

²¹ For to me to live is Christ, and to die is gain.

Father in the name of Jesus, I thank you and I pray that my ferventness and zeal for you will increase day by day, Father I thank you that for me to live is Christ, and to die is gain, but it is your will for me now, that I abide here for the furtherance of the gospel, in Jesus name, Amen.

²² But if I live in the flesh, this is the fruit of my labour: yet what I shall choose I wot not.

Father in the name of Jesus, I thank you for the grace of Jesus Christ in me to share the gospel with others, therefore, I look for an opportunity or create an opportunity to share the gospel of Jesus Christ, in season and out of season, planting, watering, and God gives the increase, in Jesus name, Amen.

²³ For I am in a strait betwixt two, having a desire to depart, and to be with Christ; which is far better:

Father in the name of Jesus, I thank you that to be absent from the body is to be present with you, Father I thank you that the believers are groaning for the redemption of their bodies, in Jesus name, Amen.

²⁴ Nevertheless to abide in the flesh is more needful for you.

Father in the name of Jesus, I thank you that it is your will that I abide here for the sake of the furtherance of the gospel, in Jesus name, Amen.

²⁵ And having this confidence, I know that I shall abide and continue with you all for your furtherance and joy of faith;

Father in the name of Jesus, I thank you that as I abide here, it is for the furtherance of the gospel and joy of faith, Father you are keeping me here for the gospel: that is while you did not take me away from the earth the moment I accepted Jesus Christ into my heart, in Jesus name, Amen.

²⁶ That your rejoicing may be more abundant in Jesus Christ for me by my coming to you again.

Father in the name of Jesus, I thank you for the joy of leading people to the saving knowledge of Jesus Christ, Father I pray that I will continue to share the gospel in season and out of season, I pray that I will share the gospel of my Lord Jesus Christ, whom I am not ashamed of, whether other believers share the gospel with sinners or not, Father I thank you that your zeal is eating me, in Jesus name, Amen.

27 Only let your conversation be as it becometh the gospel of Christ: that whether I come and see you, or else be absent, I may hear of your affairs, that ye stand fast in one spirit, with one mind striving together for the faith of the gospel;

Father in the name of Jesus, I thank you and I pray that my conversation and my lifestyle will be pleasing to you, I pray that I will live a life of non-compromise, I pray that Jesus Christ will be glorify in me and through me in word and in deed, in Jesus name, Amen.

²⁸ And in nothing terrified by your adversaries: which is to them an evident token of perdition, but to you of salvation, and that of God.

Father in the name of Jesus, I thank you that by your grace I will not be terrify by my adversaries in anything, but I will stand firm and be bold in my relationship with Christ, for in Christ I do live, move and have my being, in Jesus name, Amen.

²⁹ For unto you it is given in the behalf of Christ, not only to believe on him, but also to suffer for his sake;

Father in the name of Jesus, I thank you that I do believe in Jesus and I am not ashamed nor am I afraid to suffer for his sake, Father I thank you that when I am reproach for the name of Christ, the spirit of glory and of God will rest upon me: on their part he is evil spoken of, but on my part he is glorified, Father I thank you that I am crucified with Christ, nevertheless I live, yet not I but Christ, and the life which I do now live in the flesh, I live by the faith of my Lord Jesus Christ, who love me and gave his life for me, in Jesus name, Amen.

[30] Having the same conflict which ye saw in me, and now hear to be in me.

Father in the name of Jesus, I thank you that your grace is sufficient for me, Father I thank you that your grace does abound in me in suffering, in Jesus name, Amen.

CHAPTER TWO

¹ If there be therefore any consolation in Christ, if any comfort of love, if any fellowship of the Spirit, if any bowels and mercies,

Father in the name of Jesus, I thank you for the consolation in Christ, Father I thank you for the comfort of love in Christ, Father I thank you for the fellowship of the Spirit in Christ, Father I thank you for the bowels and mercies in Christ, above all, Father I thank you that Christ is in me, in Jesus name, Amen.

² Fulfil ye my joy, that ye be likeminded, having the same love, being of one accord, of one mind.

Father in the name of Jesus, I thank
you and I pray that believers will hungry and taste after righteousness, I pray
that your word will prevail in my life
and in the life of fellow believers, I
pray that we will not seek after vainglory but seek to please you in all we
say and do, Father I pray that your love
will abound among fellow believers,
Father I pray that you will tear down
spiritual wall created by men, which is
producing division among fellow believers, in Jesus name, Amen.

**[3] Let nothing be done
through strife or vainglory;
but in lowliness of mind let
each esteem other better
than themselves.**

Father in the name of Jesus, I thank
you and I pray that I will never seek
attention for myself but I will give all
the attention to you, Father I pray that I
will seek to please you alone in all I do

in word or in deed, and not seek to please anybody, Father I pray that I will see people the way you see people, Father I pray that I will never devalue who I am and whom I am, Father I pray that I will not devalue any human being, regardless of their status in society because you created them in your own image and likeness, in Jesus name, Amen.

⁴ Look not every man on his own things, but every man also on the things of others.

Father in the name of Jesus, I thank you and I pray that whatever I do in word or in deed that Christ will be glorify, I pray my lifestyle will be encouragement to other believers in Christ, in Jesus name, Amen.

⁵ Let this mind be in you, which was also in Christ Jesus:

Father in the name of Jesus, I thank
you for the mind of Christ which you
have given me, I boldly and una-
shamed declare to the unseen and seen
world that I do have the mind of
Christ, I dare to think Bible thoughts, I
dare to think and act on the word of
God, I dare to act in any situation as
Jesus Christ will act in that situation,
in Jesus name, Amen.

⁶ Who, being in the form of God, thought it not robbery to be equal with God:

Father in the name of Jesus, I thank
you that I think it not robbery for me to
dare to speak boldly who you said I
am, I dare to say I am born again, I am
a Christian, my name is written down
in the Lamb's book of life, I am
washed in the precious blood of Jesus
Christ, God Almighty is my Father, I
belong to God, I am heir of God and
joint-heir with Christ Jesus, I am sanc-

tified, I have been baptism in water, I am baptism in the Holy Ghost, I do speak in other tongues has the Spirit gives me utterance, I am God's ambassador in Christ Jesus, Jesus Christ represent me in the heavens and I do represent Jesus Christ on this earth and in this world, God is my very own Father and I am his very own child, in Jesus name, Amen.

7 But made himself of no reputation, and took upon him the form of a servant, and was made in the likeness of men:

Father in the name of Jesus, I thank you for the humility my Lord Jesus taught me and the example he left for me, Father I pray that I will not seek recognition but I will always seek to please you in all my ways and in all I do, in Jesus name, Amen

⁸ And being found in fashion as a man, he humbled himself, and became obedient unto death, even the death of the cross.

Father in the name of Jesus, I thank you for your love for me that led Jesus Christ to the cross, Father I thank you that I am crucified unto the world and the world is crucified unto me, in Jesus name, Amen.

⁹ Wherefore God also hath highly exalted him, and given him a name which is above every name:

Father in the name of Jesus, I thank you that you do reward obedience, Father I thank you that you highly exalted Jesus Christ and gave him a name which is above every name, Father I thank you that the name of Jesus still hold the same power as it did in the past, Father I thank you that the name of Jesus is above every circumstance, every condition, every situation, every sickness, every disease, every discomfort, every problem, every lack, and every sin, in Jesus name, Amen.

10 That at the name of Jesus every knee should bow, of things in heaven, and things in earth, and things under the earth;

Father in the name of Jesus, I thank you that at the name of Jesus every knee must bow, of things in heaven, and things in earth, and things under the earth, Father I thank you for Jesus Christ who has given me his name to use in pray and against all kinds of evils, in Jesus name, Amen.

11 And that every tongue should confess that Jesus

Christ is Lord, to the glory of God the Father.

Father in the name of Jesus, I thank you that you have ordained it and it will come pass that every tongue will and must confess that Jesus Christ is Lord to your glory, Father I do confess Jesus Christ is Lord, in Jesus name, Amen.

[12] Wherefore, my beloved, as ye have always obeyed, not as in my presence only, but now much more in my absence, work out your own salvation with fear and trembling.

Father in the name of Jesus, I thank you and I pray that I will not only act on your word when I am among believers, but also act on your world when other believers are not around,

Father I pray that I will live a life that always bring glory to you, in Jesus name, Amen.

¹³ For it is God which worketh in you both to will and to do of his good pleasure.

Father in the name of Jesus, I thank you that you are the one that is at work in me, both to will and to do your good pleasure in me, I do deliberately yield my spirit, soul and body to the working of your Holy Spirit that dwell in me mightily, Father I thank you that Christ in me the hope of glory, in Jesus name, Amen.

¹⁴ Do all things without murmurings and disputings:

Father in the name of Jesus, I thank you that everything begat his or its kind, Father I thank you that I was begat by you, Father thank you that you are Love and I am love, Father I thank you and I pray that whatever I do in word or in deed, I will do it to your glory, Father I pray that I will only be motivate by love, in Jesus name, Amen.

¹⁵ That ye may be blameless and harmless, the sons of God, without rebuke, in the midst of a crooked and perverse nation, among whom ye shine as lights in the world;

Father in the name of Jesus, I thank you for the precious blood of Jesus, I thank you for redemption, I thank you that my salvation is full, I thank you for the baptism of the Holy Spirit, I thank you for the prosperity of my spirit, soul and body, Father I thank you for material prosperity so that I do not have to beg and bring reproach to your name. Father I thank you that Jesus Christ does manifest in me and through me everywhere I go, I do take the name of Jesus with me everywhere I go, the name of Jesus Christ is glorify in me and by me in this present evil world, and sinners do acknowledge Jesus Christ in me, in Jesus name, Amen.

16 Holding forth the word of life; that I may rejoice in the day of Christ, that I have not run in vain, neither laboured in vain.

Father in the name of Jesus, I thank you that I am not ashamed of the gospel of Jesus Christ, for it is your power unto salvation to everyone that believe, Father I thank you that I am a believer, Father I thank you that my sharing the gospel of Jesus Christ and my living by your word will never be in vain, in Jesus name, Amen.

¹⁷ Yea, and if I be offered upon the sacrifice and service of your faith, I joy, and rejoice with you all.

Father in the name of Jesus, I thank you and I pray that when I suffer for preaching the gospel of my Lord Jesus Christ that your sufficient grace will overtake me, and that I will joy and rejoice, in Jesus name, Amen.

¹⁸ For the same cause also do ye joy, and rejoice with me.

Father in the name of Jesus, I thank you that I have cast my lot for you, to live and died for you, I will not turn to the right hand or to the left, my heart and eyes are fix on you alone, for you alone is the God of my salvation, in Jesus name, Amen.

¹⁹ But I trust in the Lord Jesus to send Timotheus short-

ly unto you, that I also may be of good comfort, when I know your state.

Father in the name of Jesus, I thank you for the people your Spirit led me to witness Jesus to in the past, Father I pray that each of them that are born again will remain steadfast in Christ Jesus, in Jesus name, Amen.

[20] For I have no man like-minded, who will naturally care for your state.

Father in the name of Jesus, I thank you that my trust is in you, Father I trust you and I believe that you are working every situation for my good because you love me, Father I thank you that my trust is not on the organized religion nor unorganized, my trust is not in people but my trust is in you alone, O! God of my Salvation, in Jesus name, Amen.

²¹ For all seek their own, not the things which are Jesus Christ's.

Father in the name of Jesus, I pray that Jesus Christ will always be my first priority in everything I do, Father I pray that I will never compromise my relationship with Jesus Christ, Father I pray that I will never be ashamed of Jesus Christ, Father I pray that everyone that I come in contact with or that hear about me, will know about my complete and total commitment to Jesus Christ, in Jesus name, Amen.

²² But ye know the proof of him, that, as a son with the father, he hath served with me in the gospel.

Father in the name of Jesus, I thank you for those that I led to Christ by your Spirit and I did disciple, Father I pray that each of them will stay faithful to their relationship with you, Father I pray that none of them will be carry way by religion or false doctrine, in Jesus name, Amen.

23 Him therefore I hope to send presently, so soon as I shall see how it will go with me.

Father in the name of Jesus, I thank you for my involvement in the great commission, Father I thank you that I am not ashamed of the gospel of my Lord Jesus Christ, for it is your power unto salvation to everyone that believes in Jesus Christ, in Jesus name, Amen.

24 But I trust in the Lord that I also myself shall come shortly.

Father in the name of Jesus, I thank you for those that I disciple in the past, Father I thank you for bringing some of them across my path for me to see their steadfast love for you and their relationship with you, Father I am grateful to you for the fruit of my labour in the gospel of Jesus Christ, in Jesus name, Amen.

25 Yet I supposed it necessary to send to you Epaphroditus, my brother, and companion in labour, and fellowsoldier, but your messenger, and he that ministered to my wants.

Father in the name of Jesus, I thank you for fellow ministers of the gospel, Father I pray that each of us will fulfill your call in our life while will work together in love, faith, holiness and righteousness, in Jesus name, Amen.

26 For he longed after you all, and was full of heaviness, be-

cause that ye had heard that he had been sick.

Father in Jesus name, I thank you for your love in me towards the brethren, Father I thank you for your grace that abide in me to pray for the sick, Father in the name of Jesus, I pray every believer will rise up to their spiritual responsibility to know that you have anointed each of them to pray for the sick, in Jesus name, Amen.

^{27} For indeed he was sick nigh unto death: but God had mercy on him; and not on him only, but on me also, lest I should have sorrow upon sorrow.

Father in the name of Jesus, I thank you for Jesus Christ who carried all my sickness, diseases, grief and pains upon himself, that I dead to sin, should live unto righteousness by whose stripes I am healed, Father I thank you that you sent your word to me and healed me and delivered me from destructions, Father I thank you that with long life will you satisfy me and show me your salvation, Father I thank you that your word is health and life to my flesh, in Jesus name, Amen.

[28] I sent him therefore the more carefully, that, when ye see him again, ye may rejoice, and that I may be the less sorrowful.

Father in the name of Jesus, I thank you and I pray that by your grace I will not only share the gospel with people and lead the ones you have obtained to eternal life to you, but also to follow up on those I have led to you, as Apostle Paul did in the book of acts, in Jesus name, Amen.

²⁹ Receive him therefore in the Lord with all gladness; and hold such in reputation:

Father in the name of Jesus, I thank you that your word said we should receive one another even as Christ received us, Father I pray that I will receive fellow Christians as Christ has received me, in Jesus name.

³⁰ Because for the work of Christ he was nigh unto death, not regarding his life, to supply your lack of service toward me.

Father in the name of Jesus, I thank you that you are working and doing your own good please in me, Father I pray that I will not abuse my body in ministry, I pray that I will deliberately have a daily adequate sleep and rest, plenty of water, adequate food when I am not fasting, and never yield to any form of worry of any kind within and outside, in Jesus name, Amen.

CHAPTER THREE

¹ Finally, my brethren, rejoice in the Lord. To write the same things to you, to me indeed is not grievous, but for you it is safe.

Father in the name of Jesus, I thank you that your word is truth, Father I thank you that your word is for edification, admonishment, and for correction, Father I thank you that the entrance of your word gives light, Father I thank you that your word is a lamp unto my feet and a light unto my path, in Jesus name, Amen.

² Beware of dogs, beware of evil workers, beware of the concision.

Father in the name of Jesus, I thank you for your word that warn me about false teachers, false teachings, and false doctrines, Father I do receive your word and act boldly on your word, in Jesus name, Amen.

³ For we are the circumcision, which worship God in the spirit, and rejoice in Christ Jesus, and have no confidence in the flesh.

Father in the name of Jesus, I thank you that not of work should anyone boast, for salvation is only in the name of Jesus, Father I thank you that I do believe in the name of Jesus and I have accepted Jesus Christ into my heart, therefore I can call you my very own Father because I am your very own child. Father my boasting is in you alone, in Jesus name, Amen.

⁴ Though I might also have confidence in the flesh. If any other man thinketh that he

hath whereof he might trust in the flesh, I more:

Father in the name of Jesus, I thank you for your word, Father I thank you that I do not compare myself to anyone neither do I measure myself by anyone, Father I thank you that your word said that I do not wrestle with flesh and blood, Father I pray that I will always live by your word, I pray that I will not give myself to distraction, in Jesus name, Amen.

5 Circumcised the eighth day, of the stock of Israel, of the tribe of Benjamin, an Hebrew of the Hebrews; as touching the law, a Pharisee;

Father in the name of Jesus, I thank you for the blood of Jesus Christ that purchased my salvation, Father I thank you for good works but good works could not save me, Father I thank you that religion could not save me, Father I thank you that my salvation is completed in Christ Jesus, in Jesus name, Amen.

[6] Concerning zeal, persecuting the church; touching the righteousness which is in the law, blameless.

Father in the name of Jesus, I thank you that I will not crucify Jesus Christ again, Father I thank you that I do not live in sin, Father I thank you that I do receive fellow believers in Christ as Jesus Christ has received me, in Jesus name, Amen.

[7] But what things were gain to me, those I counted loss for Christ.

Father in the name of Jesus, I thank you that my good living could not bring salvation to me, Father I thank you for Jesus Christ who brought salvation to me, Father I thank you that there is neither salvation in any other: for there is none other name under heaven given among men, whereby we must be saved. Father I thank you that salvation is only in the name of Jesus, in Jesus name, Amen.

⁸ Yea doubtless, and I count all things but loss for the excellency of the knowledge of Christ Jesus my Lord: for whom I have suffered the loss of all things, and do count them but dung, that I may win Christ,

Father in the name of Jesus, I thank you that being born again not of corruptible seed, but incorruptible seed, Father I thank you that Christ in me, the hope of glory, Father I thank you that your word is sweeter than honey to my taste, Father I thank you that you are supreme over everything in my life, in Jesus name, Amen.

⁹ And be found in him, not having mine own righteousness, which is of the law, but that which is through the faith of Christ, the righteousness which is of God by faith:

Father in the name of Jesus, I thank you that I do not have righteousness which is of my own, Father I thank you that I do not obtain righteousness by my works, I thank you that you made Jesus Christ unto me righteousness, Father I thank you that Jesus Christ is my righteousness, in Jesus name, Amen.

¹⁰ That I may know him, and the power of his resurrection, and the fellowship of his suf-

ferings, being made conformable unto his death;

Father in the name of Jesus, I pray that I will always hungry for fellowship with you, Father I thank you that you know that there are a lot of distraction in this present world, but I trust you that you will reveal to me every distraction that try to interfere with my fellowship with you, Father I thank you that your grace in me is sufficient for me to let go of any distraction to our fellowship, Father I want to know you more daily, Father I pray our fellowship, your word, prayers, and I acting on your word will always be my daily highest priority, Father I pray the power of the risen Lord Jesus which is in me, will daily manifest in me and through me, in Jesus name, Amen.

[11] If by any means I might attain unto the resurrection of the dead.

Father in the name of Jesus, I pray that you will reveal to me daily the power that raise Jesus Christ from the dead, Father I thank you that the same power does dwell in me now, because I am a believer, in Jesus name, Amen.

[12] Not as though I had already attained, either were already perfect: but I follow after, if that I may apprehend that for which also I am apprehended of Christ Jesus.

Father in the name of Jesus, I thank you for Jesus, Father I thank you that my greatest desire in life is to know you more and more every day, and to know your perfect will for me more and more every day, to long and hungry for you more and more every day, an hungry which nothing on earth can satisfy, in Jesus name, Amen.

¹³ Brethren, I count not my- self to have apprehended: but this one thing I do, for- getting those things which are behind, and reaching forth unto those things which are before,

Father in the name of Jesus, I thank you that I have not obtain that you will have me to obtain, I thank you for the past, but I am not satisfy with my present relationship with you, for I am hungry for more of you, as a Deer pant after the water, so my soul does long for you, I do deliberately forget those things which are behind and reaching forth to those things which are before, I pray that I will not camp on past achievement in you, and never to be satisfy in my knowledge of you and in my relationship with you, but to keep pressing forward daily in you, in Jesus name, Amen.

¹⁴ I press toward the mark for the prize of the high calling of God in Christ Jesus.

Father in the name of Jesus, I thank you for your word, Father I thank you that your word is sweeter than honey to my taste, Father I thank you that I do esteem your word above my necessary food, Father I pray that I will always hungry for your word, Father I pray that I will always look unto Jesus, not circumstance, Father I thank you that the things I do see are temporary and the things I do not see are eternal, in Jesus name, Amen.

¹⁵ Let us therefore, as many as be perfect, be thus minded: and if in any thing ye be otherwise minded, God shall reveal even this unto you.

Father in the name of Jesus, I thank you that I do enjoy spending time with you daily, Father I thank you that I do enjoy our fellowship, Father I thank you that I am a doer of your word, Father I thank you that whatever I do not know, you will reveal to me, in Jesus, name, Amen.

¹⁶ Nevertheless, whereto we have already attained, let us walk by the same rule, let us mind the same thing.

Father in the name of Jesus, I thank you that I do act on those things you revealed to me, Father I thank you that I am a doer of your word, Father I thank you that I do fellowship with other believers without compromising your word, in Jesus name, Amen.

¹⁷ Brethren, be followers together of me, and mark them which walk so as ye have us for an ensample.

Father in the name of Jesus, I pray that I will always search the scripture to see that those things which I heard are so, regardless of who did the preaching, sermon, message, speech, and testimonies. Father I thank you that I do abide in you and your word does abide in me, in Jesus name, Amen.

[18] (For many walk, of whom I have told you often, and now tell you even weeping, that they are the enemies of the cross of Christ:

Father in the name of Jesus, I thank you that all things are naked before you, Father I thank you that no one can deceive you, Father I thank you that anyone that hear your word and refuse to do it, deceive himself or herself, Father I thank you that I am a doer of your word, in Jesus name, Amen.

¹⁹ Whose end is destruction, whose God is their belly, and whose glory is in their shame, who mind earthly things.)

Father in the name of Jesus, I thank you that you are my God, Father I thank you that my belly is not my God, Father I thank you that I do bring my body under subjection to your word, Father I thank you that I do take delight in fasting, Father I thank you that I am risen with Christ and I do seek those things that above, where Christ is seated at your right hand, I do set my affections on things above, not on things on the earth and my life is hidden in Christ, in Jesus name, Amen.

²⁰ For our conversation is in heaven; from whence also we look for the Saviour, the Lord Jesus Christ:

Father in the name of Jesus, I thank you that thus I am bodily present here on earth, my way of living is govern from heaven by you, Father I thank you that I am not in the flesh but I am in the spirit, Father I thank you that I am led by your Spirit, in Jesus name, Amen.

²¹ Who shall change our vile body, that it may be fashioned like unto his glorious body, according to the working whereby he is able even to subdue all things unto himself.

Father in the name of Jesus, I thank you that Christ is all in all, I thank you that it is Christ that will change my body unto his glorious body, in Jesus name, Amen.

CHAPTER FOUR

¹ Therefore, my brethren dearly beloved and longed for, my joy and crown, so stand fast in the Lord, my dearly beloved.

Father in the name of Jesus, I thank you for fellow believers that are living by your word. Father I thank you that I always rejoice to meet fellow believers, Father I pray you will strengthen each believers I come in contact with, I pray that their inner man will be strengthen by the same power that raise Jesus Christ from the dead, in Jesus name, Amen.

² I beseech Euodias, and beseech Syntyche, that they be of the same mind in the Lord.

Father in the name of Jesus, I thank you and I pray that fellow believers will be of the same mind, I pray that we that believed in Jesus Christ and confess him as our Saviour and Lord will allow the word of God to prevail in every fabric of our lives as the word prevailed in the Church of Ephesus, in Jesus name, Amen.

³ And I intreat thee also, true yokefellow, help those women which laboured with me in the gospel, with Clement also, and with other my fellowlabourers, whose names are in the book of life.

Father in the name of Jesus, I thank you for calling me into the ministry of my Saviour and Lord Jesus Christ, Father I pray that I will always be faithful to you and the calling, Father I pray for all those you called into the ministry:

both male and female will be faithful
to you who called them, in Jesus name,
Amen.

⁴ Rejoice in the Lord always: and again I say, Rejoice.

Father in the name of Jesus, I thank
you that your word said I should rejoice in the Lord always: again I
should rejoice. Father I thank you that
I am your obedient child and I am a
doer of your word, therefore, I settle it
in my heart to rejoice in the Lord always, no matter the circumstance
around me and no matter how I feel,
your grace is sufficient for me, and
you are working everything for my
good, for I do love you and I am called
by you according to your purpose, in
Jesus name, Amen.

⁵ Let your moderation be known unto all men. The Lord is at hand.

Father in the name of Jesus, I thank you that I am a living and written epistle, read by all I come in contact with, Father I thank you that none live to himself or herself, Father I thank you that I do not live to myself, but I do live for him, who loved me and gave himself for me, Father I thank you that I am not ashamed of the gospel of Christ, for it is your power unto salvation to everyone that believes, Father I thank you that I am crucified unto the world and the world is crucified unto me, Father I thank you that I do bear the mark of Jesus Christ in and on me everywhere I go, in Jesus name, Amen.

[6] Be careful for nothing; but in every thing by prayer and supplication with thanksgiving let your requests be made known unto God.

Father in the name of Jesus, I thank you that you do not want me to worry about anything, no matter what it is, Father your word said I should cast all my care upon you for you do care for me, Father in the name of Jesus I cast all my cares and worries upon you, for you do care for me, Father I thank you that you are my Father and you will take care of me, and you do take care of me, yea! I know and I am fully persuaded that my God, yes, my Father is taking care of me, Father you are my very own Father and I am your very own child, in Jesus name, Amen.

⁷ And the peace of God, which passeth all understanding, shall keep your hearts and minds through Christ Jesus.

Father in the name of Jesus, I thank you that I do pray in accordance with your word, Father I thank you that I do experience your peace that pass all understanding after I pray in accordance to your word, Father I thank you that I do deliberately and diligently cast all my cares upon you for you do care for me, Father I thank you that your peace does keep my hearts and minds through Christ Jesus, in Jesus name, Amen.

8 Finally, brethren, whatsoever things are true, whatsoever things are honest, whatsoever things are just, whatsoever things are pure, whatsoever things are lovely, whatsoever things are of good report; if there be any virtue, and if there be any praise, think on these things.

Father in the name of Jesus, I thank you that I do think on things that are true, I do think on things that are honest, I do think on things that are just, I do think on things that are pure, I do think on things that are lovely, I do think on things that are of good report, I do think on things that have virtue, and I do think on things that are praise worthy. Father I thank you that I do have the mind of Christ, in Jesus name, Amen,

⁹ Those things, which ye have both learned, and received, and heard, and seen in me, do: and the God of peace shall be with you.

Father in the name of Jesus, I pray that I will represent you very good daily everywhere I go and wherever I am, Father I pray that your name will be glorify in me and through me daily everywhere I go and in everything I do and say, in Jesus name, Amen.

¹⁰ But I rejoiced in the Lord greatly, that now at the last your care of me hath flour-

ished again; wherein ye were also careful, but ye lacked opportunity.

Father in the name of Jesus, I thank you that you are not unrighteous to forget those people who have showed me labour of love in the past for Christ sake, in Jesus name, Amen.

[11] Not that I speak in respect of want: for I have learned, in whatsoever state I am, therewith to be content.

Father in the name of Jesus, I thank you for the privilege to minister the gospel of my Saviour and Lord Jesus Christ to people, Father by your grace I do give people the opportunity to sow financially into the ministry you have given me, so that they can reap financially, in Jesus name, Amen.

¹² I know both how to be abased, and I know how to abound: everywhere and in all things I am instructed both to be full and to be hungry, both to abound and to suffer need.

Father in the name of Jesus, I thank you that you are my sufficiency, Father I thank you that you are my Lord and Shepherd, I shall not want, Father I thank you that you have given me everything pertaining to life and godliness, Father I thank you that I am satisfy with you and in you, Father I thank you that you have taught me how to be abased and how to abound in everything and in everywhere, in Jesus name, Amen.

¹³ I can do all things through Christ which strengtheneth me.

Father in the name of Jesus, I thank you that there is no limit to anything good that I cannot do, Father I thank you that I will not allow religion and tradition of men that make your word of no effect limit me from acting on your word, Father I thank you that whenever I act on your word, you are always faithful to confirm your word that I acted on, Father I thank you that I can do all things through Christ which strengthen me, in Jesus name, Amen.

¹⁴ Notwithstanding ye have well done, that ye did communicate with my affliction.

Father in the name of Jesus, I thank you and I praise you for those you used to minister to me in the time of my needs, Father I thank you for their obedient to you, Father I pray you will bless each of them bountifully, in Jesus name, Amen.

¹⁵ Now ye Philippians know also, that in the beginning of the gospel, when I departed from Macedonia, no church communicated with me as concerning giving and receiving, but ye only.

Father in the name of Jesus, I thank you for supplying all the need of those that supported me in the past, and those that are currently supporting me, Father I pray that you will reveal to them that their labour towards me was not in vain, Father I pray that you will reveal to them the truth about sowing and reaping, Father I pray that you will put in their hearts to expect harvest from you for their seeds sowed into me for the gospel, in Jesus name, Amen.

¹⁶ For even in Thessalonica ye sent once and again unto my necessity.

Father in the name of Jesus, I thank you and I am very grateful to you for those you have called to support me in the preaching of the gospel of my Saviour and Lord Jesus, Father I thank you that wherever you send me to, you have already prepare people to minister to my physical needs, in Jesus name, Amen.

¹⁷ Not because I desire a gift: but I desire fruit that may abound to your account.

Father in the name of Jesus, I pray for those who has given and still giving to the ministry you have given to me, that they will expect a reward from you in this present time and in the time to come, I pray that they will be establish in you and in your grace, in Jesus name, Amen.

¹⁸ But I have all, and abound: I am full, having received of

Epaphroditus the things which were sent from you, an odour of a sweet smell, a sacrifice acceptable, wellpleasing to God.

Father in the name of Jesus, I pray Father that you teach me how to give and how to receive, Father I pray has I read your word that I will act on it, Father I pray that I will give and receive according to your word, Father I pray that as I give and receive, that I will never draw attention to me, but to give you all the glory, for you are the One that supply all my need according to your riches in glory by Christ Jesus, in Jesus name, Amen.

[19] But my God shall supply all your need according to his riches in glory by Christ Jesus.

Father in the name of Jesus, I thank you that I am a giver and I am a receiver, Father I thank you that your word said as the world remaineth there will be seedtime and harvest, Father I thank you that I am a sower and I am a reaper, Father I thank you that whatever is true of you is true of me, because you are my very own Father and I am your very own child, Father I thank you for your grace in me that always enable me to sow good seeds, in Jesus name, Amen.

[20] Now unto God and our Father be glory for ever and ever. Amen.

Father in the name of Jesus, to you alone be all the glory, all the honour, all the worship, all the adoration, all beauty now and for ever and ever, in Jesus name, Amen.

21 Salute every saint in Christ Jesus. The brethren which are with me greet you.

Father in the name of Jesus, I pray that I will always be friendly and encouraging to fellow Christians, in Jesus name, Amen.

22 All the saints salute you, chiefly they that are of Caesar's household.

Father in the name of Jesus, I pray that your love which is shed abroad in the heart of every believer of Jesus Christ will flow from one to another, I pray that we will walk in love towards each other that the world will know that you did send Jesus Christ to the world to save the world, in Jesus name, Amen.

23 The grace of our Lord Jesus Christ be with you all. Amen.

Father in the name of Jesus, I thank you for your grace, Father I do receive your grace and I do determine by your grace to live in your grace and not to live in works, religion, traditions of men, and rituals, in Jesus name, Amen.

SOIL Foundation, Inc.

All Books can be Purchase from amazon.com, Amazon.co.uk, Amazon.de, Amazon.fr, Amazon.it, Amazon.es, Barnesandnoble.com, ebay.com, createspace.com (search: Ovbije Book)

Publication Books

All Day God

Praying the Word From the Book of Timothy

Praying the Word From the Book of Ephesians

Resurrection from the Flood

Coaching to Completion

Praying the Word From the Epistle of John

God Loves Me

God Is With Me I Am Not Afraid

Praying the Word From the Book of Galatians

Praying the Word From the Book of James

Praying the Word From the Book of Philippians

Libros en Español

**Orando la Palabra
Desde el Libro de Efesios**

Dios Me Ama

<u>Tracts:</u>

5 Things God wants you to know

Love Yourself

SONG

JESUS WILL NEVER TURN YOU DOWN

Jesus is a friend that will not turn you down

He will never leave you nor forsake you

Call on his name for he is there for you

He will save and guide you to end

He will save and guide you

REPEAT

By L. O. Ovbije

LIVING FOR JESUS

1. Living for Jesus, a life that is true,
Striving to please Him in all that I
do;
Yielding allegiance, glad-hearted
and free,
This is the pathway of blessing for
me.

   ○ *Refrain:*
   O Jesus, Lord and Savior, I give
   myself to Thee,
   For Thou, in Thy atonement, didst
   give Thyself for me;
   I own no other Master, my heart
   shall be Thy throne;
   My life I give, henceforth to live,
   O Christ, for Thee alone.

2. Living for Jesus Who died in my
place,
Bearing on Calv'ry my sin and dis-
grace;
Such love constrains me to answer
His call,

Follow His leading and give Him my all.

3. Living for Jesus, wherever I am,
   Doing each duty in His holy Name;
   Willing to suffer affliction and loss,
   Deeming each trial a part of my cross.

4. Living for Jesus through earth's little while,
   My dearest treasure, the light of His smile;
   Seeking the lost ones He died to redeem,
   Bringing the weary to find rest in Him.

By Thomas O. Chisholm

www.ingramcontent.com/pod-product-compliance
Lightning Source LLC
Chambersburg PA
CBHW060654030426
42337CB00017B/2620

* 9 7 8 1 9 4 4 4 1 1 0 5 3 *